MW00583819

Finding the Beautiful You

Lisa Cassman

Halo
PUBLISHING
INTERNATIONAL

ISBN: 978-1-61244-601-1
Library of Congress Control Number: 2017915327

Printed in the United States of America

Halo Publishing International
1100 NW Loop 410
Suite 700 - 176
San Antonio, Texas 78213
Toll Free 1-877-705-9647
www.halopublishing.com
E-mail: contact@halopublishing.com

I would like to dedicate this book firstly to my husband Steve, who believes in me and supports me with my writing. Also, to our children and grandchildren and the unconditional love they have for us.

Also, to my good friend Dee Dee who has been there for my family for many years. And Wendy; when I think of the connection I have with you and respect I have for you, I know your friendship is rare! Thank you both.

CONTENTS

INTRODUCTION

A lack of self-confidence and low self-esteem are a big problem today. Unfortunately, they lie at the root of most of our other problems as well. Lacking confidence and self-esteem affects your decision-making, relationships, and even job opportunities. Undervaluing yourself can lead to a self-fulfilling spiral of declining opportunities out of lack of confidence.

It is too important not to address. It is my hope and prayer that this book will help you do just that.

QUESTIONS TO ASK YOURSELF

1.) Are you sick and tired of feeling like a failure?

2.) Why would one person succeed and another fail?

3.) Do you feel like you are the failing one?

4.) Are you frustrated with the way you are feeling with yourself and blaming others for your problems?

5.) Do you feel trapped with no self-confidence and can't seem to find a way to like yourself?

6.) Has someone or something hurt you and you aren't sure how to deal with it?

7.) Are there certain life events that have gotten you down?

8.) Is someone or something controlling your life?

If the answer to any of these is "yes," read on. Let's find you a way to move forward and change it...

-2-
TESTING OF FAITH

Do you feel you have control over your life? Or maybe something is holding you back. Maybe something or someone has hurt you, and you're not sure that your life is in your control anymore.

How do you react to someone else's choices? Have you become a victim because of the choices someone else has made, or from certain life events?

Does anyone understand why he or she may go through trials when they do? Not all the time. There are times when we get angry with others who have hurt us, whether it is family, friends or neighbors. But in the midst of it we tend to look at God or other people to blame. Yes, people do hurt others, but it is our reaction that counts. It's about how we handle it.

We were not made to be doormats for people to walk on, so stand tall and look at yourself as a child of God. Tell yourself you are worth something and God created you to be the person He wants you to be, in His image.

The hurts we go through could also be health issues or financial. Maybe you have been through a failed marriage, had an accident, or even the death of someone close to you.

In the midst of it all, remember that God has given us many blessings. We don't always seem to take time to thank Him for them.

"Consider it pure joy, my brothers and sisters, whenever you face trials of many kinds, because you know that the testing of your faith produces perseverance. Let perseverance finish its work so that you may be mature and complete, not lacking anything. If any of you lacks wisdom, you should ask God, who gives generously to all without finding fault, and it will be given to you. But when you ask, you must believe and not doubt, because the one who doubts is like a wave of the sea, blown and tossed by the wind."

– James 1:2-6

When you are hurt, you get to make the choice to ask God to help you through it. Do you choose to hang on and say you can't forgive and allow yourself to be miserable? It's not because you can't let go, you choose not to.

God has given us free will, and wants what is best for us, and He knows that what is best for us is to look to Him in all situations, good or bad.

-3-
TAME THE TONGUE

"All kinds of animals, birds, reptiles and sea creatures are being tamed and have been tamed by mankind, but no human being can tame the tongue. It is a restless evil, full of deadly poison. With the tongue we praise our Lord and Father, and with it we curse human beings, who have been made in God's likeness. Out of the same mouth come praise and cursing. My brothers and sisters, this should not be."

– James 3:7-10

Our hearts can be cold, unchanging and unbendable. Sometimes it seems like no matter what we do, everything keeps going wrong.

Sometimes we are angry. Life itself can be hard and cold. Sometimes we want to blame others for our problems, failures or situations. But at some point everyone needs to "man up," accept your responsibilities, own your choices.

Maybe you have tried and can't do it on your own. You need help. God can help. He can bring you the change you need. You must be willing to accept change. Sometimes it hurts before there is healing. You must let go of control and give it to him. You must be willing to consciously work at it.

God loves you and His love is perfect. He alone has the tools to change your cold heart.

-4-
READ YOUR SCRIPTURE

Look up these scriptures and take down a few notes here about what they make you think and feel.

Matthew 7:12 –

Romans 5:1 –

Mark 9:23 –

-5-
MOVING FORWARD

Some healthy ways to move forward when events have gotten you down:

1.)   Talk to someone that you can trust. Although it is important not to take advice from just anyone, as they may be going through some issues themselves and could drag you down with them. They could be allowing others' issues to have control of their life. Make sure the advice you receive is from a Christian, who will also pray with you and for you.

2.)   Take care of yourself. Find something to do. Take time to read a good book, take a walk or even plant a garden. When you do find something to do, don't put working on your issues on the back burner to try and forget; they will only resurface again.

3.)   Know that if you can't change the situation, learn to accept what it is until it can be changed. Situations sometimes take time. Also don't try doing it all on your own.

4.)   Read your Bible, sing worship songs and talk to God. He will always understand how you are feeling.

5.)   Although you may want to stay in your comfort zone because it's easier there, it is worth it to do the work on yourself. Having a safe place to go and have time to yourself during this hard work on you is a good thing. Find some place that makes you feel safe and free so you are relaxed and refreshed even though you're challenging yourself to get out of your comfort zone.

Receiving professional counseling will help, but you also need to work on you. It takes time and effort on your part.

-6-
LOOKING IN THE MIRROR

"Anyone who listens to the word but does not do what it says is like someone who looks at his face in a mirror and, after looking at himself, goes away and immediately forgets what he looks like."

– James 1:23-24

How many times do we read God's word, but do not live by what it says? We all do it; we all fall short. We also look into the mirror and don't pay attention to what we see and have to look again, or even look at our watch and forget what time we just read.

An example: An elderly lady I knew one day looked in the mirror and had no idea who she was. So she hit the mirror, thinking her husband had another woman in the house. She bruised her hand, and also hurt her ego once she realized what had happened.

Allow yourself to see your true beauty when you look into the mirror. Seeing what you are worth can change your attitude and outlook on life, and your relationship with others.

-7-
JOURNAL YOUR THOUGHTS

I wish I were……

-8-
MISSING PIECE OF THE PUZZLE

What's happened? You feel like nobody cares and there is no hope.

The time has then come to move forward yourself and get up and do something about it.

Remember to take one day at a time. Nothing is so bad that you should give up. You may feel broken, but there is still part of you that is together. You can make yourself whole again.

Finding yourself is like finding the missing piece of a puzzle. You take all the pieces out and organize them, putting together the ones that best suit you first. Then when it is almost together, you may see one last thing is lost. Where do you go from here? You may search a short time or for a longer period of time, but you finally find the solution you have been longing for. You finally feel the relief of moving forward.

When at last you have the missing piece you feel whole once again.

-9-
FINDING THE BEAUTIFUL YOU

Ever wonder what it would be like to finally have the freedom of liking who you are? You have been hiding your true self for so long, you have no idea who you are. You don't even know how beautiful you really are.

Imagine being bottled up with carbonation. You finally have it opened and the bubbly self you once were overflows again with confidence. The time has come: find that beautiful you that you deserve to know.

Allow no one and nothing to stand in your way and hold you back from who you really are.

Take control of your own life!

-IO-
WHAT CAN CAUSE LOW SELF-WORTH?

Regret:

Do you have regrets? Maybe you wanted to go to college, and you never did. Or you moved and wish you hadn't... What can you change to move forward from what you didn't do?

Anger:

Work on where your anger is coming from. What caused it and how can you change what you had no control over?

Fear:

What are you afraid of? Are you afraid of failure because it has happened before? Go out and deliberately do what scares you. Are you afraid of speaking in a group? Do you want to go back to school? Go and do it!

Unforgiveness:

Has someone hurt you so badly that you can't find it in your heart to forgive? Maybe it is yourself you need to forgive. Write a letter if you don't feel you can go to the person. I once had someone go to her mother's grave to tell her she forgave her. The relief she had after was exactly what she needed, but don't wait until it is too late.

Believing lies, from yourself or others, will cause low self-worth and affect your decision- making. Don't live up to someone else's expectations. It's ok to disagree with others; it's how you react that matters.

-II-
READ YOUR SCRIPTURE

Look up these scriptures and take down a few notes here about what they make you think and feel.

Proverbs 12:25 –

Nahum 1:7 –

Psalm 30:5 –

-12-
TAKE ACTION

What can happen if you lose motivation? Life in general can become a struggle. Your poor self-worth gets you down.

Something or someone can get in your way of getting stronger. It could be an illness, or even a family member not communicating with you. Maybe you feel you can't afford to purchase something you have wanted for a while.

Losing motivation may cause depression. You may be discouraged, worried, or even have doubt about the path of your life, or doubt in your relationships with others. Loneliness is another issue, as you may want to be by yourself and feel as if the whole world is against you.

With the emotional setbacks, it could eventually lead to physical issues such as migraines, stomach pain, or even heart issues. It may even cause weight loss or gain.

Do you worry? Replace worry with prayer. Worrying won't change what is going to happen.

"Therefore I tell you, do not worry about your life, what you will eat or drink; or about your body, what you will wear. Is not life more than food, and the body more than clothes? Look

at the birds of the air; they do not sow or reap or store away
in barns, and yet your heavenly Father feeds them. Are you
not much more valuable than they? Can any one of you by
worrying add a single hour to your life?

And why do you worry about clothes? See how the flowers of
the field grow. They do not labor or spin. Yet I tell you that not
even Solomon in all his splendor was dressed like one of these.
If that is how God clothes the grass of the field, which is here
today and tomorrow is thrown into the fire, will he not much
more clothe you—you of little faith? So do not worry, saying,
'What shall we eat?' or 'What shall we drink?' or 'What shall
we wear?' For the pagans run after all these things, and your
heavenly Father knows that you need them. But seek first his
kingdom and his righteousness, and all these things will be
given to you as well. Therefore do not worry about tomorrow,
for tomorrow will worry about itself. Each day
has enough trouble of its own.''

– Matthew 6:25-34

So how can you take control of your own life? TAKE ACTION!
Not taking action is like starting a car, and not putting it in gear
to go somewhere. Don't lose yourself in the fear of not getting
anywhere. Do what frightens you... If you want a vacation,
save money for it, or if you what to write a book, sit down and
write your thoughts.

Nothing will happen if you don't take action and move
forward.

-13-
DREAMS

Dreams are something we all have. What you do with them is another thing, as you may want something and feel like you can't have it.

If you really want something, find a way to get it. Sometimes it may not be reality, but you won't know unless you try. It is not called failing, it is called doing your best. And something else may arise from it. Don't let setbacks stop you from what you deserve.

Learn to focus on what you do have, and take the little things and make them into big things. If you start to see the beauty in what you have, you will appreciate so much more.

Whether it is in relationships or in material things, we don't need a lot to make us happy and content.

Don't be so comfortable in your life that you want to stop and won't move forward.

-14-
NEEDING STRENGTH

"I can do all things through Him who gives me strength."

– Philippians 4:13

You are stronger then you think or feel you are. Many times it is in the power of the mind. You are what you hear or think. We can feel the power of weakness come over us. We all make mistakes, it doesn't mean we have to pay for them the rest of our lives. Never quit, if you fall pick yourself back up. Today is a new day!

You can give to others but you don't need to be taken advantage of. You can listen, but yet don't lose your voice. You don't need to give in to others to make them happy. Be yourself and love, but don't be used. Show your true self, with your head held high. Don't let anyone have control over you to the point that you lose your identity just to try and please them.

When a situation arises that you feel overwhelmed with and life seems to pass you by, you try to heal on your own. It doesn't work that way. Stop playing God. People often think they deserve the punishment, but where does the true source of pain come from? Satan, and his wounds and the lies he tells us.

If you are in doubt, take that small step forward to move on. Remember life isn't fair, but it is still good. Always think of your life as yours, don't compare it to others.

God has such wonderful plans for us, and we just don't always want to listen and move forward. Take a moment and feel his presence to see what you can do for the glory of God.

-15-
JOURNAL YOUR THOUGHTS

If I could I would......

-16-
FEELING LONELY?

Do you need to be around people and no one comes to see you? That can affect how we feel about ourselves, especially if something has happened and we feel lonely. Life is too precious and goes by too fast; don't let it pass you by.

Take the time to go see someone who may need some people in their life. Or maybe do volunteer work to be around others doing that will make a difference for you and someone else. Helping others can make you feel better too. If something or someone won't make time to come see you, making the time to see them will help you feel needed.

Don't be too hard on yourself, and try to find the best in who you are.

-17-
TAKING RESPONSIBILITY

It is not our job to try and fix someone else, or take responsibility for their actions. You need to be responsible for you, and the choices you have made. You can love them and support them, but their choices aren't yours.

There may come a time when others want to blame you for something they chose to do. Most of the time, nobody can make you do something.

When a person starts making bad choices because of something that has happened to them, they should find ways to deal with that and let it go to start the healing process.

What are some behaviors that can stem from being hurt?

-18-
TAKE CARE OF YOURSELF

Life has its way of helping those who may need it—even using you. You may not even know that you have the power to make someone's day.

I once had someone with anxiety come to see me. In the beginning she didn't realize the difference she felt while seeing me. She came in a few times before realizing she felt safe and relaxed while she was coming in for a treatment. She had physical issues constantly but none of them appeared while she was with me. This is one example of how I was able to help her and she was willing to receive and accept it. Her words were "I come in for me." This was her time and she enjoyed the freedom she felt.

Take care of yourself. Be honest with yourself and don't believe the lies from others or the ones you tell yourself.

You woke up this morning with a choice to make it into a good day or a bad day!

Remember that emotional attacks can turn to physical attacks. What are some things that can cause anxiety attacks for you? What are some things you can do to help get through an anxiety attack?

-19-
JOURNAL YOUR THOUGHTS

I wish I could change......

-20-
TAKE A BREATHER

Do you ever get mad at someone because of something that has happened? Something that is totally out of anyone's control? Maybe something happened at work and you were tired so now what?

Has someone hurt you so you put up your defenses before they could do it again? Maybe so that *nobody* could ever do it again.

You take it out on the one you are closest to. You may get angry and frustrated.

Also, maybe someone has done something that wasn't "the norm", and you want to try change them. Why should we take it upon ourselves to act as if we are better that that person? You should work on you first, and then share your frustration so you don't say anything you regret.

Taking it out on someone else— or even getting angry at yourself— isn't going to make the situation any better.

If you see that you may be getting upset, take a breather. Focus on the positive, not what could happen, but hasn't yet.

-2I-
TRUST

"Trust in the LORD with all your heart
and lean not on your own understanding;
in all your ways submit to him,
and he will make your paths straight."

– Proverbs 3:5-6

Trusting others is sometimes really hard to do as too many times, we get hurt. Some people may have hurt you over and over again.

Sometimes it isn't even directed at us, it is something that that person has done to harm themselves or someone else.

God wants to teach you how to trust again by trusting in Him first. If you lean on what you know and stay in your comfort zone, you won't get too far with seeing the love others can have for you.

Because someone has hurt you so much, it is easy not to trust anyone else. You may feel the world is against you and will take advantage of what you have to offer.

Trust in God before you trust in any person. Then the trust for others will gradually follow.

-22-
GOD HAS THE ANSWER

"This is what the LORD says, he who made the earth, the LORD who formed it and established it—the LORD is his name: 'Call to me and I will answer you and tell you great and unsearchable things you do not know.'"

– Jeremiah 33:3-4

This says it all: how many times do we have something happen and not know what to do? If we would just trust God, we'd know that He will give us an answer, maybe not right away but He will as soon as it is in His time. Open your heart to what has and hasn't happened yet.

The choice is yours, but to move forward it is important to forgive those who have hurt you.

Sometimes someone may keep doing the same hurtful thing over and over. It is up to you if you want to allow that person to keep up with it— as long as it is not harmful.

Pick your battles, but stay strong and not defeated by the enemy!

-23-
CONTROL OF YOUR LIFE

Take control of your life, once and for all.

What is it that you want to do with your life? Do you want to go back to school, find a different job?

Maybe you are alone and want a partner in your life. You won't find one if you aren't doing anything about it. Once you have taken care of you—you're finding your self-worth and moving forward—then you are ready to invite someone else into your life.

If you carry baggage with you it is a lot more work to have the trust that you deserve in your relationship.

Are you lonely? Find that self that you so deserve and work on the goals of moving forward.

Take action! Don't wait until tomorrow to find yourself.

You could plan on getting in touch with someone, and then by the time you actually make plans actions, they may be gone and it could be too late.

Don't wait for yourself to find worth; do it before it is too late.

-24-
READ YOUR SCRIPTURE

Look up these scriptures and take down a few notes here about what they make you think and feel.

Psalm 34:5 –

Psalm 37:23-24 –

Psalm 46:1 –

-25-
BE YOURSELF

Are you serious about healing or changing? You can talk-the-talk, all while not really wanting to move forward. Maybe you are scared that you will go through something that makes you uncomfortable. That fear is okay to feel, but don't let it stop you. Knowing that the end is worth it, will bring you further along in getting past all the fear of taking action. Take a deep breath, and remind yourself that life can and will be better.

Take care of you— not for anyone but yourself. Don't pretend to be someone you are not. You are only lying to yourself, covering your feelings and dealing with life in a more negative way.

Allow others to share their input, and teach you ways to let go. Don't try doing it all on your own. You have a wonderful future as soon as you leave the past behind...

It is called the past for a reason.

-26-
GIVE IT ALL TO GOD

*"Do not let any unwholesome talk come out of your mouths,
but only what is helpful for building others up according to
their needs, that it may benefit those who listen. And do not
grieve the Holy Spirit of God, with whom you were sealed for
the day of redemption. Get rid of all bitterness, rage and anger,
brawling and slander, along with every form of malice. Be kind
and compassionate to one another, forgiving each other,
just as in Christ God forgave you."*

– Ephesians 4:29-32

I understand these verses, because I was so unhappy with my
life I wanted others to be miserable with me. I took what I could
and started finding faults with everyone I came in contact with.
I didn't want anyone else to be happy or successful.

I finally had to look at myself with all I was doing and give my
life totally to God. I had only given part of me in the beginning
and still hung onto so much hurt and anger over life events that
had happened to me.

Nobody deserves the negative talk. Nobody deserves to be
called names and put down. Usually when someone is finding
faults and hurting someone, they are hurting themselves. So

let's find a way to get past this and move on to having a positive attitude.

In this day, so many hold grudges and choose not to make peace. Don't be one of them.

-27-
WAYS TO LET GO OF BITTERNESS, ANGER AND SLANDER

1.) Find the source: what has caused you to become so angry at someone?

2.) Is it really just something they have done? Or is it because something they did has triggered the emotions from something that has happened to you in the past?

3.) Is it something you have done— and don't like yourself because of it?

4.) Stop getting even.

5.) Pray for peace and healing.

-28-
CHANGES IN LIFE

Are you thankful for what you have?

Life can change in an instant. Yes, it is a human reaction to pray when something bad is about to happen or is happening. We may take what we have for granted, not thinking life can change in a moment's time with or without notice.

Imagine watching your house going down in flames and there is nothing you can do, someone close to you on their death bed, or even going to work one day and realizing the company is no longer there. You never know when you will have a challenge or a change in your life.

The weather is a crazy thing. If you think about the fires out west or Hurricane Harvey in Texas or Irma in Florida, would you be prepared to leave your house and belongings behind, knowing this may be the end of most or all of your material items you have worked so hard for?

We never know when storms of life will come up. Be prepared for anything. We shouldn't have to worry, but know there are some things in life we have no control over.

What would you do in a time of facing something so big? What would you do, knowing you can't control the situation? How have you prepared your heart for these types of changes?

-29-
JOURNAL YOUR THOUGHTS

How do you want others to see you?......

-30-
SILENCE

When you hear the words "silence is golden," what are your reactions or thoughts on this?

When someone is silent, why are they silent? Sometimes it may be better to say nothing than to hurt someone, but then there comes a time when someone is silent for all the wrong reasons. Like when you are mad at someone and giving them the silent treatment. The problem is but that doesn't help when you should be talking it out.

Keeping silent can hurt you by bringing you into withdrawals and keeping it all bottled in. You may become stressed or have anxiety attacks, which could lead to other health issues.

Just like when the paint on the walls is chipping and instead of fixing it, you cover it up. It just continues to chip. You keep finding excuses and covering up your pain. It doesn't go away, it will continue to surface in other areas of your life.

-31-
NEVER GIVE UP

While trying to accomplish something that you have had as a goal for many years, things may come up that try to stop you from reaching your finish line.

Years ago as I was taking courses to get my pastor's license, I would get frustrated when I couldn't afford my next course. I never once told anyone when I wasn't able to afford the next stage of the course, and yet a dear lady from church once in a while handed me a gift of money and told me specifically that it was for my studies.

A couple weeks after I had earned my license, she became ill and found she had cancer. She only survived a few days after the surgery.

I felt so blessed that she shared a passion for what I was called to do. Through her, God encouraged me to never give up no matter the challenges on the way.

-32-
UNSEEN FAITH

"Now faith is confidence in what we hope for and assurance about what we do not see."

– Hebrews 11:1

Only you can open your eyes to what God is doing and saying to us. It may seem like nothing is going our way, but where is your hope and where does it come from?

God's grace is sufficient for you. You are strong enough to face what He has and hasn't done for you. You are strong enough to face the day.

We are all broken and damaged, but the love God has for us can give us new hope and the faith we need to see what is ahead of us going forward.

You can either take what life has given to you and let it make you bitter, or you can take what life has given to you and let it make you better. It is your decision.

If you are feeling bitter, do something about it. Only you can. Don't let it define you. You don't have to be afraid to change.

Remember: God is just a prayer away. You are never alone.

-33-
PRAYER LIFE

"Rejoice always, pray continually, give thanks in all circumstances; for this is God's will for you in Christ Jesus."

– 1 Thessalonians 5:16-18

"If you believe, you will receive whatever you ask for in prayer."

– Matthew 21:22

How do you pray for others?

"Lord, it's me again. I want you to change my husband. I don't like what he's doing. I am angry at him. He makes me so mad."

Does this prayer seem selfish? How about this one:

"Lord, please help me to understand my husband and be more willing to share with him my needs. Help me to be thankful and to show him my appreciation of him."

Maybe you pray with repetition, repeating the same prayer every day.

So many make it about themselves, having little consideration of what someone else may be going through.

God invites you to have a conversation with Him; talk to Him and not at Him. Make it personal. Thank God for what He has done and what He has given you.

-34-
READ YOUR SCRIPTURE

Look up these scriptures and take down a few notes here about what they make you think and feel.

Psalm 136:1 –

Philippians 4:4 –

1 Peter 5:7 –

-35-
JUDGMENT OF OTHERS

We have all had a time in our lives when we look at someone and think they deserved what they got...

"Keep on loving each other as Christian brothers. Do not forget to be kind to strangers and let them stay in your home. Some people have had angels in their homes without knowing it. Remember those in prison. Think of them as if you were in prison with them. Remembering those who are suffering because of what others have done to them. You may suffer the same way."

– Hebrews 13:1-3

Going forward after bad choices in our lives isn't always easy, but it can be done. Remember, nothing is too hard for God and nothing is so bad that he won't forgive us. We just need to change our behaviors and make better choices.

It is so easy to judge others without knowing what or how they feel. We can be so selfish and talk about others negatively behind their backs, or look at their faults. Can you honestly look in the mirror and say you have reached out to those hurting, or do you go to others and talk about them? We don't understand why people do what they do, but reaching out to say you care is a big step closer to what Jesus is teaching in scripture.

I remember once someone telling me that we need to look at it as if we could be in the same situation. We never know what life may bring us from day to day. Don't look back on what it should have been, just take one day at a time and move forward.

> *"Get up! Stand on your feet! I have chosen you to work for me..."*
>
> *– Acts 26:16*

Our dreams, like the person you are judging, may be replaced with the harsh reality of compromise, failure, and lack of hope. But with God we can make it through anything.

-36-
WHAT IS LOVE?

The definition of love can be various things:

1.) Intense affection for one another

2.) A strong feeling of attraction

3.) 1 John 4:16: "God is love."

"Love is patient, love is kind..." – 1 Corinthians 13:1

Now let's put "God" in for the word "love."

"God is patient, God is kind..."

In the book of Genesis chapter 1, verses 26-27, it tells us we are made in the image of God. Put your name in place of "love." Are you patient? Are you kind? Can you read that to say you are like God? Although none are perfect, God wants us to follow Him.

Have you been lied to? Have you been deceived, or felt neglected? Maybe forgotten or left behind? Rejection hurts. Before you get even, get honest with yourself. Have you neglected God?

At some point we may have someone turn their back on us. We know how much it hurts.

Quit focusing on what others have done to you and start focusing on what God has done *for* you and you can start loving others.

Jesus had friends betray him. Some even abandoned him.

Can you imagine the nails that pierced Jesus' flesh? Each breath He took would have hurt. Every muscle and nerve in His body was in pain.

Remember the last words Jesus said; not to get even, not to lash out back, not to hurt others. No matter what they had done, Jesus still loved them.

Can you forgive even if you have been hurt?

Think right now how much love can change your life, guiding you through the trials and sowing the seed of faith. Each time we hurt Jesus, he loves enough to forgive. How strong is your faith and love for God? Strong enough to do the same?

Remember God is love. And Jesus' last words dying on the cross were, "Father, forgive them."

-37-
JOURNAL YOUR THOUGHTS

How do you think God sees you?......

-38-
INSTRUCTIONS FOR BEING HAPPY

There are those people that seem to be happy and cheerful no matter what life throws their way. Do you ever wonder why you can't be happy like that?

1 Thessalonians offers us 16 ways we should live in the last days. These are our final instructions for being happy.

Verse 16 says, "Rejoice always!" which is interpreted, "Be glad; be delighted!"

How can we be happy when something comes into our life that upsets us? We can look to Christ and be glad we wake up each morning to face the day. Try looking on the bright side. Nothing is really as bad as we make it out to be.

Verse 17 says, "Pray without ceasing." Talk to Jesus and have a friend in Him. He can be our best friend and we should share our thoughts— good and bad— with Him. Know that He hears every word and knows your every thought anyway.

Verse 18 says, "In everything give thanks." Express your gratitude. Has something in your life happened and you feel you can't give thanks? Start by thanking Him for something that you are still thankful for. Whether it is an accomplishment or something positive that's happened in your life.

Verse 18 continues, "For this is the will of God." It is the will of God that we be happy, not miserable and suffering. It is not easy to always rejoice, pray without ceasing, and give thanks for everything. But it is possible with God.

What will you choose today? Be happy with a smile or go on living with a frown on your face?

-39-
A TRUE FRIEND

Do you know what a true friend really is? The word "Friend" has been defined as: "someone you have affection and regard for who is neither relative nor lover."

Is there anyone in your life that has regard for you all the time? We all have disagreements, and find out real soon that no one is perfect. When we expect people to be perfect, we set ourselves up for failure.

The one true friend we have is Jesus. He stands by us at all times. We don't understand why people will hurt us, but Jesus still knows our heart.

"Brothers and sisters, do not slander one another. Anyone who speaks against a brother or sister or judges them speaks against the law and judges it. When you judge the law, you are not keeping it, but sitting in judgment on it. There is only one Lawgiver and Judge, the one who is able to save and destroy. But you—who are you to judge your neighbor?"

– James 4:11-12

This is a powerful passage to learn from. We have no right judging others. It is between that person and God.

A young man once talked to me about his beliefs. He grew up going to church and youth group. He soon got into witchcraft and as he talked to me about it, I just listened. He knew what I believed in, and he finally asked me, "Aren't you going to tell me I am going to hell?" I replied back, "That is between you and God." He then asked me to be praying for him.

Sometimes your actions are more powerful than words. Remember the phrase, "What would Jesus do?"

"So in everything, do to others what you would have them do to you, for this sums up the Law and the Prophets."

– Matthew 7:12

Living by this scripture will make you a great friend. And you will always have Jesus as a friend too.

-40-
READ YOUR SCRIPTURE

Look up these scriptures and take down a few notes here about what they make you think and feel.

Hebrews 10:36 –

2 Chronicles 15:7 –

-41-
VENGEANCE IS NOT YOURS

"Be kind and compassionate to one another, forgiving each other, just as in Christ God forgave you."

– Ephesians 4:32

Forgiving someone who has hurt you is one of the hardest things to do as a Christian. Forgiving doesn't mean you have to trust them again right away. It means that you cleared your conscience with God and have allowed Him to take control of the situation. It doesn't mean you have to be best friends. It means you can know that when you are singing worship songs, that you can sing from your heart and soul, not just say the words.

"Do not take revenge, my dear friends, but leave room for God's wrath, for it is written: 'It is mine to avenge; I will repay,' says the Lord."

– Romans 12:19

There have been many times I have wanted to get even with someone for something that they had said or done to me. The words, "I will get even" have come to mind. I even spoke the words to someone, and later had to ask for forgiveness. She said no one had ever asked for her forgiveness before, knowing she was in the wrong. But so was I, for being vengeful.

Love others with kindness. Show the true meaning of what living for Christ is.

-42-
LIVE IN HARMONY

*"Love must be sincere. Hate what is evil; cling to what is good.
Be devoted to one another in love. Honor one another above
yourselves. Never be lacking in zeal, but keep your spiritual
fervor, serving the Lord. Be joyful in hope, patient in affliction,
faithful in prayer. Share with the Lord's people who
are in need. Practice hospitality.*

*Bless those who persecute you; bless and do not curse. Rejoice
with those who rejoice; mourn with those who mourn. Live in
harmony with one another. Do not be proud, but be willing to
associate with people of low position. Do not be conceited.*

*Do not repay anyone evil for evil. Be careful to do what is right
in the eyes of everyone. If it is possible, as far as it depends on
you, live at peace with everyone."*

— Romans 12:9-18

If you don't agree with what someone else is doing and start
saying mean things about them, you are no better than them
and what they may represent to you.

Saying things that aren't true about someone and creating lies
about situations is just as bad. This is when we need to look
at the bright side and start rejoicing for what we do have. Be
patient and loving and pray faithfully.

Help those who need help, without expecting anything in return and do not boast about what you have done.

Do not start an argument, as that will also put you in a position of paying evil with evil. Keep focusing on what is right in the Lord.

Humble yourself before the Lord, and he will lift you up.

When we have a low self-worth, we tend to focus on the negative and not what positive things we should be doing according to scripture.

-43-
CURTAIN OF LIFE

"Therefore, brothers and sisters, since we have confidence to enter the Most Holy Place by the blood of Jesus, by a new and living way opened for us through the curtain, that is, his body, and since we have a great priest over the house of God, let us draw near to God with a sincere heart and with the full assurance that faith brings, having our hearts sprinkled to cleanse us from a guilty conscience and having our bodies washed with pure water. Let us hold unswervingly to the hope we profess, for he who promised is faithful. And let us consider how we may spur one another on toward love and good deeds, not giving up meeting together, as some are in the habit of doing, but encouraging one another—and all the more as you see the Day approaching."

– Hebrews 10:19-25

We are free to enter a new and living way that Jesus has opened for us. How do you see the light from outside inside of your home? You open the curtains. The new curtain to life is through Christ's body. We can be cleansed, taking all the guilt and shame away, by being washed of our sins by the blood of Jesus.

Being a child of God, washed in His blood, your sins are forgiven. Here are some commands for us:

    1.) Draw near to him, with a sincere heart.

Zacheaus is an example of this. He took tax payers' money but when he came to believe the Lord, he gave everything back and more.

2.) Having our hearts cleansed of a guilty conscience.

Are you honest with God, giving your all to Him? Do you have a clean heart? Pure conscience? You are either living for God or not— there is no in-between…

> *"So, because you are lukewarm—neither hot nor cold—I am about to spit you out of my mouth."*
>
> *– Revelation 3:16*

3.) Have unwavering faith.

God is faithful. Have you lost your direction of what God would like you to do? Trust in Him and He will guide you, not in your way or your timing— but in His!

4.) Urge others towards love and good works.

Can you honestly say you are a good influence on those around you?

5.) Go to church.

He does not say where or when, He says don't stay away from church meetings. Do you see more of this in the day coming? The end times are near; we should act as though each day is the last. We need to be fed and watered by God's Word and fellowship with the saints.

Now you know how a Christian should live.

The scripture above goes on to say in verses 26-27, if we go on sinning after we know the truth, there is nothing but fear as we wait for judgment and the terrible fire that will destroy all those who live against God.

Are you willing to take the chance of not being with Jesus on the judgment day or will you make your life right today?

-44-
JOURNAL YOUR THOUGHTS

What would you like to change about yourself?......

-45-
PRAY FOR WISDOM

"This is why I have never stopped praying for you since I heard about you. I ask God that you may know what He wants you to do. I ask God to fill you with the wisdom and understanding the Holy Spirit gives."

– Colossians 1:9

If you tell someone that you will pray for them, take a moment right then to do it, so they know the prayers are being said.

God wants us to do His work according to His will. We each have talents and gifts that have been given to us. No one can be used for His glory on their own, just as in the church we need to work together to make it a church. Where will you go with the gifts God has given you? More times than not we end up with road blocks, but God gets us through them to continue on the journey to do what needs to be done for Him.

Be willing to do what God wants in your life, because what He wants and what we want may not be the same. Continue to pray and ask for God's will. Be patient and never give up. He will show you what is right for you.

"Pray for us. Our hearts tell us we are right. We want to do the right thing always."

– Hebrews 13:18

When God has work for us to do He will show us, and we will feel it and know in our heart it is from Him.

Take time each day to pray, read the Bible, worship, and fellowship with other Christians so you may hear from God to see what His will is in your life. Our pride may get in the way or you may not want others see that you are having a difficult time, but don't be afraid to ask for prayer.

God's way is the only way to get through life, so ask for His will to be done and for Him to show you the direction He wants you to go. Follow His path and be guided by Him to know what is right for you.

-46-
FIND YOUR GIFT

Each one of us has a different gift, or a function, but none of us are better or worse than the other. Some may feel that since they are more successful or may be more talented in hobbies or sports, that they are better, so then we start to pick winners and losers.

Romans 12:3-8 describes how we are different and have different functions which all work together as one. We are to focus on the talents we have to serve others. Use whatever gift you have for God's ministry.

"We have different gifts, according to the grace given to each of us. If your gift is prophesying, then prophesy in accordance with your faith; if it is serving, then serve; if it is teaching, then teach; if it is to encourage, then give encouragement; if it is giving, then give generously; if it is to lead, do it diligently; if it is to show mercy, do it cheerfully."

– Romans 12:6-8

We can find fulfillment in being ourselves and using the gift God has given us. Then you are no longer more important than your neighbor, you are both just as important as each other. Do you appreciate one another for who you are, without making anyone feel different?

Gods view on others is to work together with cooperation not competition. This is the first step to building a loving community.

If you continue reading in Romans 12, you will find how a Christian community is to love. Love must be sincere, devoted to one another in brotherly love, living in harmony with one another and overcoming evil with good.

Share with Gods people who are in need. Be willing to associate with people who are different from you. Without us reaching out to and caring for one another, the church will fall short of what God has intended.

-47-
PLANTING SEEDS

*"While a large crowd was gathering and people were coming
to Jesus from town after town, he told this parable: 'A farmer
went out to sow his seed. As he was scattering the seed, some
fell along the path; it was trampled on, and the birds ate it up.
Some fell on rocky ground, and when it came up, the plants
withered because they had no moisture. Other seed fell among
thorns, which grew up with it and choked the plants. Still other
seed fell on good soil. It came up and yielded a crop,
a hundred times more than was sown.'*

*When he said this, he called out, 'Whoever has ears
to hear, let them hear.'*

*His disciples asked him what this parable meant. He said,
'The knowledge of the secrets of the kingdom of God has been
given to you, but to others I speak in parables, so that,*

*"though seeing, they may not see;
though hearing, they may not understand."*

*This is the meaning of the parable: The seed is the word of
God. Those along the path are the ones who hear, and then the
devil comes and takes away the word from their hearts, so that
they may not believe and be saved. Those on the rocky ground
are the ones who receive the word with joy when they hear it,
but they have no root. They believe for a while, but in the time
of testing they fall away. The seed that fell among thorns stands
for those who hear, but as they go on their way they are choked
by life's worries, riches and pleasures, and they do not mature.
But the seed on good soil stands for those with a noble and
good heart, who hear the word, retain it, and by
persevering produce a crop.'"*

— Luke 8:4-15

76

This is to show us that Jesus knows that things happen and we may not stay strong enough to keep following Him.

We can let so many life events get to us and we walk away. Sometimes something happens and we cover it up with things that shouldn't be part of our lives, because we are not strong enough to give it to Jesus. We want to hang on to it ourselves.

We can give our life to Jesus, and live for Him because everything is going great. But what happens when a situation arises that isn't what we had in mind? Either the rocks or the weeds get in the way.

-48-
JOURNAL YOUR THOUGHTS

Who do you feel is the real you?......

-49-
GOD'S PLANS FOR YOU

" 'For I know the plans I have for you,' declares the LORD,
'plans to prosper you and not to harm you, plans to
give you hope and a future'."

– Jeremiah 29:11

We can plan our future, and have so much going for us, when all of a sudden it all comes to a stand-still, and we don't know where to go from there.

Life isn't always what we want or expect it to be. We have to realize not to expect anything to be perfect.

Anything can happen. It could be a death, an illness, or an accident of some sort. It could be a job loss or failed marriage. How are you going to react to it and how do you go forward?

God has a plan for you. He doesn't want you to hurt. If you hang on to the hurt, it is harming you more.

Give it all to Him. He wants to carry it for you so you don't have to anymore.

-50-
STANDING FIRM

"Humble yourselves, therefore, under God's mighty hand, that he may lift you up in due time. Cast all your anxiety on him because he cares for you.

Be alert and of sober mind. Your enemy the devil prowls around like a roaring lion looking for someone to devour. Resist him, standing firm in the faith, because you know that the family of believers throughout the world is undergoing the same kind of sufferings.

And the God of all grace, who called you to his eternal glory in Christ, after you have suffered a little while, will himself restore you and make you strong, firm and steadfast. To him be the power forever and ever. Amen."

– 1 Peter 5:6-11

God wants to lift you out of the pit. Do you have anxiety or stress in your life? Think about what can cause it. It could be many things.

Has someone hurt you and it continues to surface with certain life events? Take time to write a letter and without sending it, say how you feel about what has happened. Find someone you can trust and read it to them.

80

I have had many hard things happen to me that I could be dwelling on, but God has placed in my heart the willingness to choose to forgive and let go. I wouldn't be where I am today if I hadn't moved forward. In the process of being hurt, I hurt others and to move forward, I had to ask forgiveness from them. I was blaming others for my choices, yet, really, I was to blame. It also may be you are blaming yourself for something that happened to you.

Having the faith is what will take you through the sufferings. Open your eyes to what is going on around you. It is not only you that is having a hard time.

The best feeling is to forgive and to be forgiven. It is such a relief and restoration. Nobody is perfect and nobody can make you choose to forgive and move forward. Only you can do that.

-51-
TRUTH WILL SET YOU FREE

"To the Jews who had believed him, Jesus said, 'If you hold to my teaching, you are really my disciples. Then you will know the truth, and the truth will set you free.'"

– John 8:31-32

Powerful words! The truth is that we can be set free.

So many want to try to heal on their own. We can take the time and search, we can quickly focus on what could happen, but without having the faith and trust in Jesus, we find ourselves covering up so many life events and making more out of it then necessary.

To walk yourself through this journey of life after something difficult has happened, here are a few steps to take to help you heal. Will you heal completely? That is up to you and what you choose to do. You may still have little things that trigger something in you because of what's happened, but keep your head up and eyes fixed on the prize. If you fall down, pull yourself right back up.

1.) Recognize where the pain is coming from. What is the source of pain?

2.) Talk about it. Are you covering up the pain with something else?

3.) Realize there is hope. Whatever the circumstance, there is always hope. Look at what you do have, not just what has happened to you.

4.) If it is someone who has hurt you, take the energy you have and pray for them. If they have said something to hurt you, remember the lyrics of the song: "You can talk about me all that you please. I will talk about you down on my knees."

5.) Do not feel guilty; it isn't your fault.

6.) If it is something you have done, ask for forgiveness and then forgive yourself.

7.) Find healthy ways to cope.

8.) Give it to Jesus. He wants to carry it for you.

-52-
JOURNAL YOUR THOUGHTS

What are your strong points?......

What are your weak points?......

-53-
COURAGE

"Do not be afraid or discouraged because of this vast army.
For the battle is not yours, but God's."

– 2 Chronicles 20:15

Where does your hope come from? Do you have complete faith
and trust in God? If you don't, how can you have hope and trust
in family, friends, or anyone? God wants you to take the trust
and see that he will not abandon you, nor will he keep you down
when you feel that there is no way through what you're facing.

Knowing that he will make you strong and bring you to your feet
is what he wants from you. The battle can be won, and you can
and will be able to move forward with courage and strength.

The victory is the Lord's and the battle will be won.

Are you going to win with the Lord and be who you were created
to be? Or are you going to keep allowing someone or something
else to control your life and who you are?

Give it all to Him today and allow Him to carry it for you.

-54-
HABITS OF A STRONG, CONFIDENT PERSON

1.) A strong, confident person does not allow anyone or anything else to control their life. They have the ability to take control of the situation.

2.) They wake up each day with an attitude of, "It is a new day and nothing will happen that I can't handle."

3.) They appreciate the success of others and don't look at themselves as a failure.

4.) They appreciate the little things in life and are thankful for what they do have.

5.) They walk with their heads held high, but do not boast!

6.) No matter how they feel, they get up and get dressed and go on with their day.

7.) They know that beauty isn't just on the outside. It is also what is in someone's heart and mind.

As you grow into the strong, confident person you are, will you have an occasional bad or off day? Of course, you will. But you know that you can get passed whatever life throws at you. You will soon be back on track. Nobody and no situation is perfect.

-55-
PUT YOUR PAST BEHIND YOU

"You were taught, with regard to your former way of life, to put off your old self, which is being corrupted by its deceitful desires; to be made new in the attitude of your minds; and to put on the new self, created to be like God in true righteousness and holiness.

Therefore each of you must put off falsehood and speak truthfully to your neighbor, for we are all members of one body. "In your anger do not sin": Do not let the sun go down while you are still angry, and do not give the devil a foothold. Anyone who has been stealing must steal no longer, but must work, doing something useful with their own hands, that they may have something to share with those in need.

Do not let any unwholesome talk come out of your mouths, but only what is helpful for building others up according to their needs, that it may benefit those who listen. And do not grieve the Holy Spirit of God, with whom you were sealed for the day of redemption. Get rid of all bitterness, rage and anger, brawling and slander, along with every form of malice. Be kind and compassionate to one another, forgiving each other, just as in Christ God forgave you."

– Ephesians 4:22-32

This being said, are you aware that God wants you to put your past behind you? That means all things are to be made new; a new self and a new mind.

The verses speak for themselves.

I had to let go of so much hurt. I had to forgive others and myself. I am a new creation, a brand new man. The old is behind me. Each day is new with God. Is my life perfect? No. Will I still be hurt and even hurt others? Yes. But I want to live my best for what God has in store for me.

I am moving forward to the person God created me to be with new love and forgiveness.

-56-
A PERSONAL PRAYER

"For God so loved the world, he gave his one and only begotten son that whosoever believes in him shall not perish but have everlasting life."

– John 3:16

Pray and ask Jesus to be your Savior, to guide you through your healing process.

An example of a prayer: "Jesus, I ask You now to come into my life. Forgive me of my sins, and help me to heal and trust that You will get me through this hurt and pain. Take my life and use me to do Your works, and live the way You want me to. I no longer belong to the world, but to You— the One who has given Your life for me."

Make your prayer personal and talk to Him as if He is sitting next to you, as He always will be.

-57-
JOURNAL YOUR THOUGHTS

Do you feel you should become someone else to be liked? Why or why not?......

-58-
ADDITIONAL NOTE SPACE

CPSIA information can be obtained
at www.ICGtesting.com
Printed in the USA
FFOW05n0800201017